Victor Farmington Library
15 West Main Street
Victor, NY 14564

50 THINGS YOU DIDN'T KNOW ABOUT CANADA

Written and Illustrated by Sean O'Neill

RED CHAIR PRESS

Egremont, Massachusetts

50 Things You Didn't Know About is produced and published by Red Chair Press: www.redchairpress.com

FREE lesson guide at www.redchairpress.com/free-activities

Publisher's Cataloging-In-Publication Data

Names: O'Neill, Sean, 1968- author, illustrator. | O'Neill, Sean, 1968- 50 things you didn't know about (Series)

Title: 50 things you didn't know about Canada / written and illustrated by Sean O'Neill.

Other Titles: Canada

Description: Egremont, Massachusetts : Red Chair Press, [2024] | Interest age level: 006-009. | Includes index. | Summary: With 50 Things You Didn't Know About Canada, young readers will discover highlights of Canada's history and First Nations culture, as well as marvel at its modern traditions and incredible natural scenery. And no book about Canada is complete without exploring unique aspects of food, daily life and hockey.--Publisher.

Identifiers: ISBN: 978-1-64371-386-1 (library hardcover) | 978-1-64371-387-8 (softcover) | 978-1-64371-388-5 (ebook) | LCCN: 2023940795

Subjects: LCSH: Canada--History--Juvenile literature. | Canada--Description and travel--Juvenile literature. | Canada--Social life and customs--Juvenile literature. | CYAC: Canada--History. | Canada--Description and travel. | Canada--Social life and customs. | BISAC: JUVENILE NONFICTION / People & Places / Canada. | JUVENILE NONFICTION / Travel.

Classification: LCC: F1008.2 .O54 2024 | DDC: 971--dc23

Copyright © 2025 Red Chair Press LLC
RED CHAIR PRESS, the RED CHAIR and associated logos are registered trademarks of Red Chair Press LLC.

All rights reserved. No part of this book may be reproduced, stored in an information or retrieval system, or transmitted in any form by any means, electronic, mechanical including photocopying, recording, or otherwise without the prior written permission from the Publisher. For permissions, contact info@redchairpress.com

Printed in the United States of America

0524 1P F24CG

TABLE of CONTENTS

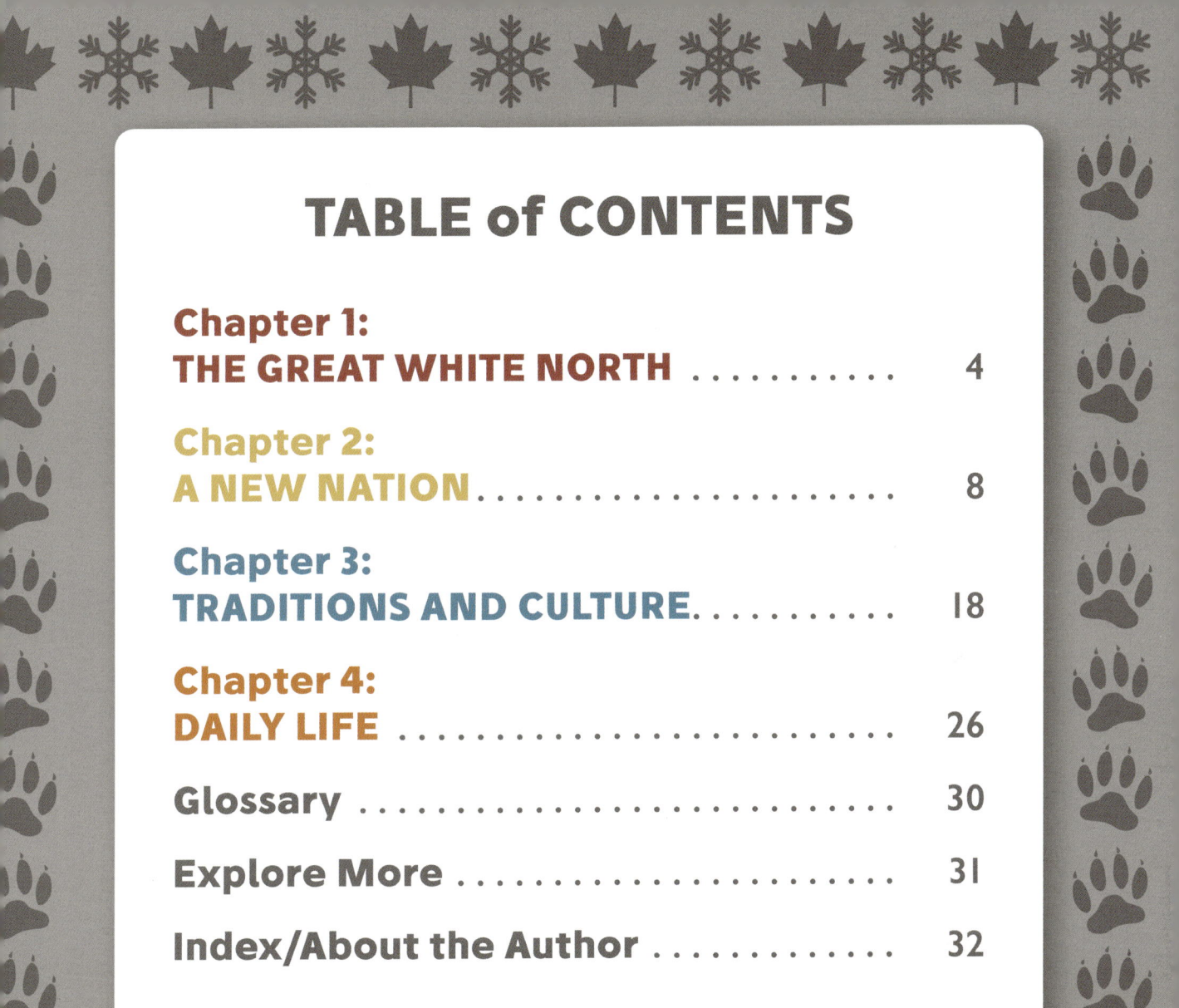

Chapter 1:
THE GREAT WHITE NORTH 4

Chapter 2:
A NEW NATION 8

Chapter 3:
TRADITIONS AND CULTURE 18

Chapter 4:
DAILY LIFE 26

Glossary 30

Explore More 31

Index/About the Author 32

CHAPTER 1

THE GREAT WHITE NORTH

The vast nation of Canada forms the northern section of North America. The Great White North, as it's sometimes called, does contain frozen, arctic areas, but also includes rainforest, coastal regions, mountains, and bountiful plains. There's much more to this diverse land than just snow and ice.

THE GREAT WHITE NORTH

1 At close to 4 million square miles, Canada is the second-largest country in the world by area. Canada also has the world's longest coastline–over 150,000 miles of it.

2 The name Canada is believed to be from the word kanata, which means "village" in the language of the **indigenous** Iroquois people.

3 Canada's Mackenzie River was originally called Disappointment River. Explorer Alexander Mackenzie thought it would take him to the Pacific Ocean. Instead, it led him to the freezing Arctic.

4 The town of Churchill in northern Manitoba is known as the Polar Bear Capital of the World. Residents must be on their toes, because polar bears wander through town freely eating garbage.

MMM-PIZZA!

CHURCHILL SANITATION DEPT.

5 Another example of Canadian wildlife is the moose. A moose is actually a giant **species** of deer, and males can be up to 1,400 pounds (635 kg) and have antlers up to 6 feet (about 2 meters) across.

6 A canyon in Alberta has the unusual name Head-Smashed-In Buffalo Jump. The name comes from an indigenous Blackfoot hunting technique of herding buffalo and driving them off the edge of the cliff.

THE GREAT WHITE NORTH

7 The steep cliffs of Rogers Pass in the Canadian Rocky Mountains are prone to avalanches. To solve this problem, the Canadian military has mounted howitzer cannons on each side, which they shoot to safely cause avalanches when no one is around.

8 When a new prehistoric fossil was discovered in Alberta in 1884, they cleverly named the new dinosaur *Albertosaurus*.

9 Canada's earliest inhabitants arrived about 12,000 years ago. Lower sea levels at the time allowed humans to cross from what is now Russia to North America.

CHAPTER 2

A NEW NATION

European explorers began to arrive and settle in Canada in the 15th century. They found a wild land full of wildlife and natural beauty. Of course, there were people there too. Thriving Inuit and First Nations cultures had lived there for centuries, and it would take many years before an independent, new nation would emerge.

A NEW NATION

10 The first Europeans to arrive in Canada were Norse Viking explorers led by Leif Ericsson around 1000 CE. The remains of a Viking camp L'Anse aux Meadows have been found in Newfoundland, northeastern Canada.

11 The French established a colony they called New France in 1603. The colony was profitable due to the trade in a popular new product—beaver fur!

12 The British also set up colonies in the new land. Scottish explorers claimed an area of Northwest Canada that would become the province of Nova Scotia, or "New Scotland."

13 After about 100 years of disputes with France, British rule was established in Canada in 1763. But French tradition and culture remained strong in the province of Quebec.

A NEW NATION

14 The dispute between English and French Canada would go on for 200 years. In 1969, Canada finally passed the Official Languages Act making both French and English official languages.

15 When the United States became independent from Great Britain in 1776, disputes over the border between the U.S. and Canada led to the War of 1812. In the end, neither side was victorious, and the borders remained the same.

16 Canada took a big step toward independence in 1867 with the Dominion of Canada, which gave Canada its own parliament and Prime Minister.

17 Canada was the last stop on the Underground Railroad. From the 1830s to the 1860s, more than 30,000 enslaved people made the journey north and settled in Canada.

A NEW NATION

18 A symbol of Canadian identity is the signature red coat and peaked hat of the Royal Canadian Mounted Police. The "mounties" patrolled the border with the U.S. and had a reputation for "always getting their man."

19 In 1877, Chief Sitting Bull led thousands of Sioux into Canada after the Battle of Little Bighorn. The mounties were able to negotiate a peaceful entry into the new nation and avoided conflict.

20 In 1896, gold was discovered in the far north Yukon Territory and the Klondike Gold Rush was on! Thousands of miners made their way north, but few of them found any gold.

21 Klondike gold miners didn't find much gold, but they made some other amazing discoveries: several fossils of extinct large mammals like sabre-tooth tigers and giant beavers.

22 In 1886, Prime Minister John A. MacDonald and his wife rode one of the first trains across Canada. Not that unusual, except that his wife Agnes rode most of the trip seated on the front of the locomotive!

23 Part of the border between the U.S. and Canada includes Niagara Falls. In 1901 a teacher named Annie Taylor successfully went over the falls in a barrel. Over the years 16 people have survived this feat, but many hundreds more did not.

WHO'S IDEA WAS THIS?

24 In 1931 Canada finally became an independent nation. The British monarch is still officially the head of state but has no real power to govern.

25 At the start of World War II in 1940, Canada formed the British Commonwealth Air Training Plan to train pilots from Canada, Britain, Australia, and New Zealand.

A NEW NATION

26 Canadian women were also important to the war effort. Almost 10,000 enlisted to serve in support positions as nurses, drivers, and radio operators.

27 Most people have heard of the bravery of Rosa Parks, but what about Viola Desmond? In 1946, this Black Canadian woman was arrested for refusing to move out of a whites-only section of a Nova Scotia movie theater, sparking a movement toward ending **segregation** in parts of Canada.

CHAPTER 3

TRADITIONS AND CULTURE

Canada's culture is a mixture of French, British, and Indigenous traditions, with a little bit of American pop culture mixed in for good measure. But Canadians have an identity and spirit all their own!

TRADITIONS AND CULTURE

28 The Canadian flag features a maple leaf, which has been a symbol of Canada since the 18th century. The "Maple Leaf Flag," as it's known, was adopted in 1965. It was controversial at first, because some saw it as a rejection of British identity.

29 In addition to the Maple Leaf, another national symbol of Canada is the beaver, which was made an official emblem of the country in 1975.

30 A Canadian one-dollar coin is called a "loonie" because it has a picture of a loon.

31 Off the coast of Nova Scotia is Oak Island, which contains a mysterious underground shaft, referred to as the "Money Pit." According to legend, pirate Captain Kidd buried treasure deep in the pit, but none has ever been found.

TRADITIONS AND CULTURE

32 The small city of Moose Jaw, Saskatchewan has a series of underground tunnels near the train station. During the 1920s, American gangsters used these tunnels to smuggle illegal alcohol onto trains bound for the U.S.

33 Inventor Alexander Graham Bell made significant breakthroughs on his new device for transmitting sound–what we now call a telephone–at his family home in Ontario.

34 There's perhaps no more Canadian activity than ice hockey. It's fitting, then, that the sport as we know it was invented there. The first indoor hockey game (with rules) was played in Montreal in 1875. One important new rule: use of a puck instead of a round lacrosse ball.

35 It took 80 years for another important innovation to come to hockey. In 1959 Montreal Canadiens goalie Jacques Plante strapped on a mask for the first time. Up until then goalies had been playing without any face protection.

36 The Stanley Cup, the championship trophy for NHL hockey, has been awarded to hockey champs since 1893, making it the oldest trophy for professional sports in North America.

TRADITIONS AND CULTURE

37 Canadians are very serious about hockey. In 1955 when Montreal superstar Maurice Richard was suspended for fighting, fans took to the streets and started one of the worst riots in Canada's history!

38 Baseball may be America's pastime, but on October 24, 1992, the Toronto Blue Jays became the first Canadian baseball team to win the World Series.

39 Canadian James Naismith invented basketball. Before deciding on peach baskets to catch the balls in the new game, he originally considered using boxes. Can you imagine playing "boxball"?

40 Quebec inventor Joseph-Armand Bombardier created a vehicle with an engine and steerable skis in 1922–the first snowmobile. A smaller version was meant to be called the Ski-Dog, but a printing error called it a Ski-Doo and the name stuck.

TRADITIONS AND CULTURE

41 The world's first superhero, Superman, was co-created by Canadian illustrator Joe Shuster. The fictional city of Metropolis was based on Joe's hometown of Toronto.

42 One of the world's most popular children's books, *Anne of Green Gables*, by Canadian author L. M. Montgomery, is set on Canada's Prince Edward Island.

43 Canada has contributed many superstars to the world of pop music. Rockers like Neil Young and Rush as well as pop stars Drake, Avril Lavigne and Justin Bieber are all Canadian.

CHAPTER 4

DAILY LIFE

Canada contains vast areas of wilderness and frozen tundra, but about 90% of Canadians live in cities near the U.S. border. But despite their proximity to their American neighbors, Canadians still have their own way of doing things.

DAILY LIFE

44 Canada is a diverse nation. In surveys, Canadians report more than two hundred different ethnic origins and more than one in five is an **immigrant.**

45 The CN Tower in Toronto is the tallest structure in the Western **Hemisphere** at 1,815 feet and has the world's longest metal staircase.

46 Every year the city of Calgary, Alberta hosts the Calgary Stampede, the world's biggest rodeo. The center of the city is transformed into a festival of bull riding, bronco-busting, and trick roping.

47 Edmonton, Alberta is home to the world's largest shopping mall. It's so big, they have a replica of Christopher Columbus' ship the *Santa Maria*–indoors!

48 French is still widely spoken throughout Quebec. Montreal, Quebec's largest city, is the second-largest French-speaking city in the world, after Paris, France.

DAILY LIFE

49 1.7 million Canadians identify as indigenous. These native Canadians fall into three groups: First Nations (Native North American), Inuit (Arctic), and Métis (mixed indigenous and French).

50 One language spoken in northern Canada is the Inuit language of Inuktitut. The longest word in the language is *Tuktusiuriagatigitqingnapinngitkyptinnga* which means, "You'll never go caribou hunting with me again."

Glossary

hemisphere: half of a sphere or ball: the equator divides Earth into the Northern and Southern hemispheres (or halves).

immigrant: someone who comes to a place from another place, such as from one country to a new country.

indigenous: people whose ancestors lived in a place from the earliest times.

segregation: the separation of people by groups, especially by racial groups.

species: a group of animal types that can breed or reproduce together.

Explore More

Cipriano, Jeri. *Hello Neighbor: Canada.* Red Chair Press, 2019.

Greenwood, Barbara. *The Kids Book of Canada.* Kids Can Press, 2007.

Juarez, Christine. *Canada.* Capstone Press, 2013.

Lin, Chelsea. *Weird But True Canada.* National Geographic Kids, 2018.

Van, R.L. *Canada.* Abdo Big Buddy Books, 2023.

Index

Alberta 6, 7	Montreal. 22-23, 28
Bell, Alexander Graham . . . 21	Métis. 29
Blackfoot 6	Naismith, James 23
Calgary 27	Newfoundland 9
Desmond, Viola 17	Nova Scotia 10, 20
Edmonton 28	Ontario. 21
Ericsson, Leif 9	Prince Edward Island 25
First Nations 8, 29	Quebec. 10, 24, 28
Inuit 8, 29	Rogers Pass 7
Iroquois 5	Saskatchewan 21
Mackenzie River 5	Sioux 13
MacDonald, John A. 15	Underground Railroad 12
Manitoba 6	Yukon Territory 14

About the Author/Illustrator

Sean O'Neill is an illustrator and writer living in Chicago. He is the creator of *50 Things You Didn't Know* and the *Rocket Robinson* series of graphic novels. Sean loves history, trivia, and drawing cartoons, so this project is pretty much a dream assignment. And he spent part of his childhood living in Canada.

Victor Farmington Library
15 West Main Street
Victor, NY 14564